ANIMALS ARE WILD!

STRANGE BUGS

STEVE PARKER

Gareth Stevens
PUBLISHING

Please visit our website, www.garethstevens.com.
For a free color catalog of all our high-quality books, call toll free 1-800-542-2595 or fax 1-877-542-2596

Cataloging-in-Publication Data

Names: Parker, Steve.
Title: Strange bugs / Steve Parker.
Description: New York : Gareth Stevens Publishing, 2016. | Series: Animals are wild! | Includes index.
Identifiers: ISBN 9781482450026 (pbk.) | ISBN 9781482450040 (library bound) | ISBN 9781482450033 (6 pack)
Subjects: LCSH: Insects--Juvenile literature.
Classification: LCC QL467.2 P37 2016 | DDC 595.7--dc23

Published in 2017 by
Gareth Stevens Publishing
111 East 14th Street, Suite 349
New York, NY 10003

Publishing Director Belinda Gallagher
Creative Director Jo Cowan
Editorial Director Rosie Neave
Senior Editor Claire Philip
Concept Designer Simon Lee
Volume Designer Simon Lee, Rob Hale
Image Manager Liberty Newton
Production Manager Elizabeth Collins
Reprographics Stephan Davis, Thom Allaway
Assets Lorraine King

ACKNOWLEDGMENTS:
The publishers would like to thank the following sources for the use of their photographs:
Key: (m) = main (i) = inset
Front cover: (main) Thomas Marent/Minden Pictures/FLPA, (Wild Nature animal globe) ranker/Shutterstock.com
Back cover: (top) Cathy Keifer/Shutterstock.com, (bottom) gracious_tiger/Shutterstock.com
Page 1 Christian Musat/Shutterstock.com
Pages 4–5 (clockwise from bottom left) Stephen Dalton/Naturepl.com, ARCO/Naturepl.com, James Christensen/Minden
Pictures/FLPA, Russell Cooper/Naturepl.com, Nature Production/Naturepl.com
Honeypot ant (m) Nature Production/Naturepl.com, (i) Mitsuhiko Imamori/Minden Pictures/FLPA
Praying mantis (m) Corbis/Photolibrary.com, (i) Michael Durham/Minden Pictures/FLPA
Harlequin beetle (m) Kim Taylor/Naturepl.com, (i) Stephen Dalton/Naturepl.com
Termite (m) Mitsuhiko Imamori/Minden Pictures/FLPA, (i) William Osborn/Naturepl.com
Atlas moth (m) Ronald Wittek/Photolibrary.com, (i) Michael & Patricia Fogden/Minden Pictures/FLPA
Trapdoor spider (m) A.N.T. Photo Library/NHPA
Lantern fly (m) Thomas Marent/Minden Pictures/FLPA
Giant weta (m) Louise Murray/Science Photo Library, (i) Mark Moffett/Minden Pictures/FLPA
Leaf katydid (m/i) Piotr Naskrecki/Minden Pictures/FLPA
Giant prickly stick insect (m) Imagebroker, Ingo Schulz, Imageb/Imagebroker/FLPA, (i) Chris Mattison/FLPA
Scorpionfly (m) Andy Sands/Naturepl.com, (i) Densey Clyne/Photolibrary.com
Giant centipede (m) John Mitchell/Photolibrary.com, (i) Michael D. Kern/Naturepl.com
Cicada (m) Mitsuhiko Imamori/Minden Pictures/FLPA
Two-spined spider (m) Hugh Lansdown/FLPA
Hercules beetle (m) Patti Murray/Photolibrary.com, (i) Kim Taylor/Naturepl.com
Assassin bug (m) David Maitland/Photolibrary.com, (i) Dennis Kunkel/Photolibrary.com
Peanut bug (m/i) Claudio Contreras/Naturepl.com
Blue weevil (m) Thomas Marent/Minden Pictures/FLPA, (i) Piotr Naskrecki/Minden Pictures/FLPA
Red slug caterpillar (m) Mark Moffett/Minden Pictures/FLPA, (i) Doug Wechsler/Naturepl.com
Cockchafer (m) Kim Taylor/Naturepl.com

Every effort has been made to acknowledge the source and copyright holder of each picture.
Miles Kelly Publishing apologizes for any unintentional errors or omissions.

Printed in the United States of America

CPSIA compliance information: Batch CS16GS:
For further information contact Gareth Stevens, New York, New York at 1-800-542-2595.

CONTENTS

BIZARRE BUGS: FREAKY CREATURES

We rarely notice beetles, bugs, spiders, flies and other creepy-crawlies, unless they are big and hairy – or they try to bite or sting us. But they are among the strangest of all creatures, with the most peculiar shapes, colors and features – and the most disgusting habits imaginable!

The world of bugs is a curious and dangerous place. It can be just as fast, furious and vicious as the fearsome battles we see among big predators and their victims. But compared to these great mammals, bugs are far more surprising. They have deadly venom, whirring wings, outsized body parts and many other extreme adaptations.

↗ Not all bugs are beastly – many are beautiful. The Cairns birdwing shows spectacular colors on its delicate wings.

2

WEAPONS

All spiders and centipedes, and some insects, have long fangs that deliver paralyzing venom. In other bugs the deadly dangers are at the rear end, in the shape of tail stings. Yet another tactic is venom-carrying spines and hairs almost all over the body.

DEADLY STING

1

LEGS

Walk, run, hop, leap, bound, crawl, kick, slash and hold – bugs' legs allow an enormous range of movements, not only for travel, but also for defense, attack and breeding. Insects have six of them, spiders have eight, and centipedes possess 40 or more.

INSTANT TAKEOFF

↖ With back legs twice as long as its body, a meadow grasshopper can fling itself 60 times its body length.

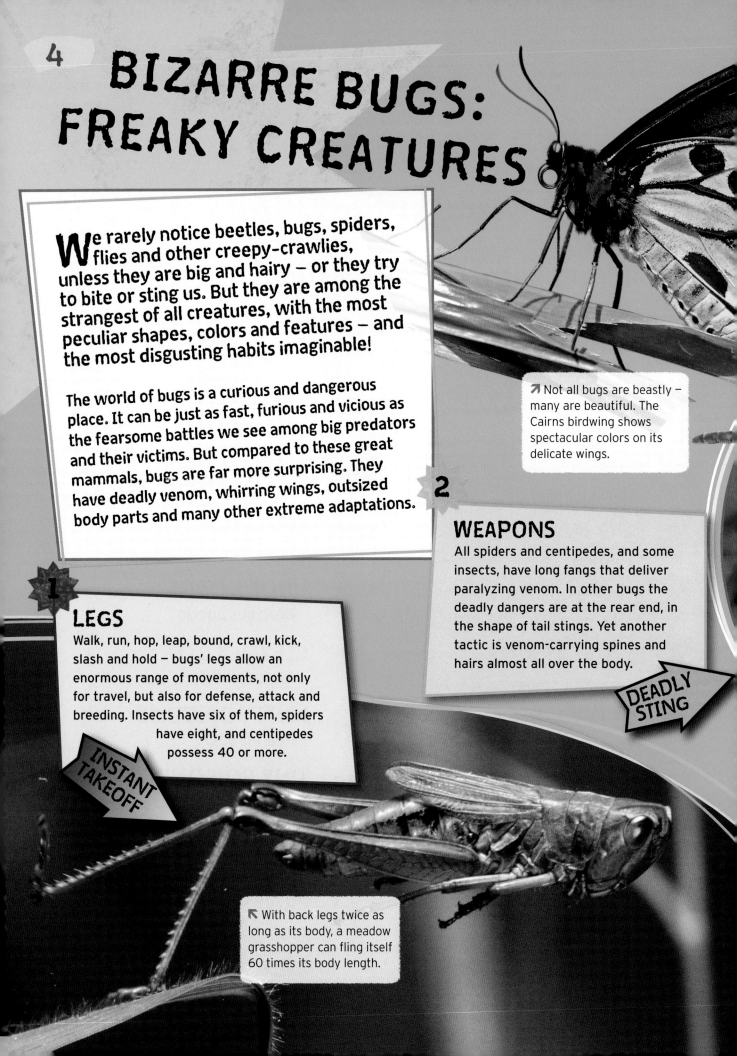

HEADS

3

In the world of bugs, strange heads are almost everywhere you look! There are delicate, straw-shaped mouths for sucking, all-purpose jaws to scrape and chew, sponge-like mouthparts that dab and soak and elaborate antennae (feelers) to catch slight scents. Bulging snouts help to impress mates and long horns are useful for tackling rival males.

HORN FACE

↓ The ferocious-looking giant hornet has a hugely powerful sting larger than a human thumb, and can be deadly to people.

↑ The rhinoceros beetle's bizarre head horn is used only to fight others at breeding time. Otherwise this bug is harmless.

← Damselflies like the banded demoiselle look fragile and dainty, but they are merciless killers of small flying insects.

FEARED FLIER

WINGS

4

Not all bugs have wings, but many species do and they take to the air for feeding and even for mid-air mating. Others avoid a flight unless the alternative is a fight, which is why insect wings have such varied designs.

Honey is packed with nourishment and sugars for energy, and is a well-known natural food source. Bees aren't the only insects that make it – honeypot ants do too, but in a very different way. Instead of storing honey in cells, these ants store it in themselves! Particular kinds of worker honeypot ants, called "repletes," eat the food brought by forager ants, convert it to honey and hang from the roof in the nest – ready to feed hungry workers when food is short.

LIVING PANTRIES

STUFFED...

The swollen repletes are so full that they cannot leave the nest or even move through its tunnels.

SUGARY SNACK...

For thousands of years, native Australians have eaten honeypot ants. They are a ready-made and sweet fast food source in the country's parched outback.

SPECIAL FEATURES

TEAMWORK: The nest foragers bring back juicy caterpillars, worms, grubs and similar morsels to feed their repletes.

PROCESSING POWER: The repletes eat the food delivered to them and process it into honey-like fluids, fats and watery liquids.

Honeypot ant

Scientific name: *Myrmecocystus* (several species)
Type: Insect – hymenoptera (bees, wasps, ants)
Lifespan: Several months
Size: "Replete" workers that store food can be up to grape-sized
Range: Dry areas, especially Australia

STAR FACT

Sometimes honeypot ants from one nest raid another nest nearby. The big-jawed workers fight their way in, kill most of the rival workers and carry the repletes back to their own nest.

STORING FOOD: The liquid food store is kept in the abdomen, which becomes so swollen that the hard, dark covering sections are pushed far apart.

FEEDER: A hungry worker asks for food by stroking the replete with its feelers and legs. The food emerges from the mouth or tail end of the replete.

When looking for prey, the triangular head of a praying mantis swivels, robot-like, on its flexible neck. Its huge eyes, which form one-third of its head, gaze while its antennae (feelers) detect a scent. The mantis sizes up its victim, edging slowly nearer and moving one leg at a time. Then… *grab!* The spiny-edged front legs flick out and snap back in a fatal hugging movement, with a meal in their powerful grip.

DEADLY EMBRACE

FLY AWAY...

Mantises usually keep their wings folded neatly along the sides of their bodies. But they can open them and flap rapidly to escape from danger.

SPECIAL FEATURES

CAMOUFLAGE: The common praying mantis is green, but flower mantises can be a variety of shades to blend in with their bright surroundings.

POSTURE: The middle and rear pairs of legs hold on firmly to plants, while the mantis' body and head lunge forwards, extending its killing range.

Praying mantis

Scientific name: *Mantis, Hierodula*
(giant mantis) and many others
Type: Insect – mantodea
Lifespan: Some kinds 5-plus years
Size: Up to 4.7 in (12 cm)
Range: Warmer woods, scrub
and bushland

BITE...

The mantis usually bites through its victim's neck to stop it struggling, then eats it right away.

STAR FACT

Large mantises tackle prey almost as big as themselves, including insects such as cockroaches and crickets, and also spiders, centipedes and even frogs, small lizards, baby birds and mice.

HEAD: Unusually for an insect, the mantis can turn its head 180 degrees to see left and right. This means its main body can stay still and undetected when hunting.

LEGS: The front pair of legs works like spiky, extending, folding flick-knives to grab prey with a snapping motion.

Named after the colorful costumes of harlequin clowns, these bugs are recognized by their bright hues and gaudy patterns. They look awkward and ungainly with long, spindly legs and even longer antennae. Yet they move with careful skill in their tropical forest home. When motionless, their coloration blends in perfectly with the jumble of mosses, lichens, fungi and flowers thriving on tree trunks and boughs.

LONG LEGS

STAR FACT

The female lays her eggs in a type of fungi on trees. Once hatched, the larvae spend a year eating and tunneling before developing into adults, and gnawing their way out of the wood to freedom.

REACH...

The elongated front legs are useful for clambering among branches – this beetle is surprisingly agile.

SPECIAL FEATURES

WINGS: The two large, tough coverings over the main body are actually front wings, which protect the smaller, delicate flight wings folded beneath.

LEGS: The patches of light color on the legs help to break up the beetle's shape. This is known as disruptive camouflage.

Harlequin beetle

Scientific name: *Acrocinus longimanus*
(giant harlequin) and others
Type: Insect – coleoptera
Lifespan: 12-18 months
Size: Body 3.1 in (8 cm), legs up to
3.9 in (10 cm)
Range: Tropical American forests

ON THE WING...

If the beetle senses danger, it launches itself into a noisy flight. It extends its feelers and legs to make sure any gaps on its flight path are wide enough to pass through.

MOUTHPARTS: This beetle is a sap-feeder, with strong, beak-shaped mouthparts that pierce the outer layers of leaves and shoots.

FORELEGS: The male's front pair of legs are even longer than the female's. The biggest males have the longest legs, which help attract females.

Termites are social insects that live in huge colonies. Some of their massive nests have more than a million inhabitants – yet most never see the light of day. These small, pale, soft-bodied insects are also known as "white ants," but they are not closely related to true ants. They live, forage, feed and breed almost entirely underground. At the heart of their colony is the queen, an egg-producing machine with a vastly swollen body full of eggs for future generations.

EGG MACHINE

STAR FACT

In some termite species, the queen lays one egg every minute for several years. She does this after mating with a male, when she is young and normal-sized.

SPECIAL FEATURES

QUEEN: The queen's head and thorax (middle), are slightly larger than a worker ant's, and the abdomen is vasty enlarged with developing eggs.

COURTIERS: Worker ants called courtiers attend to all the queen's needs including cleaning, feeding and massaging.

Termite

Scientific name: *Macrotermes* and many others
Type: Insect – isoptera
Lifespan: Workers a few months, queens 20-plus years
Size: Queens up to 7.9 in (20 cm) long
Range: Most warm habitats

FIERCE...

Soldier termites have jaws five time bigger than a worker's, and mount mass attacks on any nest invader.

SKYSCRAPER...

Some termite mounds are almost 33 feet (10 m) tall! In proportion to the size of their builders, these are five times taller than our highest skyscrapers.

FORAGERS: Foraging workers dig tunnels and collect plant food fragments such as roots, underground stems and bulbs for the whole colony.

MOUND: The tall, partly hollow mound above the underground nest works as an air-conditioning chimney to control temperature.

At dusk in the warm forests of Southeast Asia, all is quiet and still. Suddenly a large shape flits across a clearing. It is big enough to be an owl or bat, but in fact it's an insect – a female atlas moth. She has been resting in a tangle of vine leaves cloaking a tree trunk and is now out in the open, but not for long. She flies a few yards to a prominent branch, releases a mating scent and then settles down to wait for a male.

MEGA MOTH

HUGE...

The female atlas moth has a bigger wing area than any other moth, but not quite the longest wingspan. The white witch moth is one contender for the largest wingspan, at around 14 inches (35 cm).

SPECIAL FEATURES

WINGTIPS: The curved outer tip of the front wing is thought to resemble the head of a small snake, perhaps to put off predators.

BODY: In proportion to its wings, the moth's hairy body is small compared to most moths and butterflies. This moth is not a strong flier.

Atlas moth

Scientific name: *Attacus atlas*
Type: Insect – lepidoptera
Lifespan: 1 year
Wingspan: Female up to 11.8 in (30 cm)
Range: Southeast Asian forests

STAR FACT

In its adult form, the atlas moth does not eat. It survives for a week or two on food reserves built up during its caterpillar or larval stage, when it ate fruit tree leaves.

SNIFF...

The female moth gives off a mating scent or pheromone, which the male can detect hundreds of yards away with its feathery antennae.

PATTERNS: In the dark, the light-colored patches on the wings may look like the eyes of an owl or cat. This may deter predators from attacking the moth.

COLORS: The amazingly complex patterns on the moth's wings are made by mosaic-like arrangements of single-color, microscopic scales.

An unsuspecting insect wanders past some old twigs and leaves – and disappears! The pile of twigs is actually the hidden top of a trapdoor spider's burrow. The spider lays silken strands like tripwires, which are tugged by small creatures wandering past. When the spider detects a likely victim, it flings open the door, then grabs and bites the insect with its venomous fangs. Next, the prey is dragged into the spider's tunnel lair and devoured.

LETHAL TRAPPER

Trapdoor spider

Scientific name: *Anidiops, Cteniza, Ummidia* and many others
Type: Arachnid – mygalomorph
Lifespan: 10-plus years
Legspan: Up to 3.9 in (10 cm)
Range: Worldwide, mostly tropical

SNEAKY...

The spider selects items such as leaves, twigs, shells and pebbles to camouflage the trapdoor among foliage.

'STAR FACT

These spiders can be prey as well as predators. One type of wasp uses its sting to paralyze the spider, then lays its eggs inside the spider's body. The hatched larvae feed on the spider's body while it is still alive.

SPECIAL FEATURES

SILK: The trapdoor is made of woven spider silk and has a strong silk hinge on one side. The burrow is also lined with silk.

STRENGTH: Trapdoor spiders hold the door to their burrow shut using their two front legs. The other six grip the tunnel sides.

PRETTY WINGS

At night, in the darkness of the warm forest the strange–looking lantern bug is hidden. However at dawn, its shining colors and beautiful patterns are revealed in all their glory. In some species of lantern fly, the huge snout, or rostrum, can be half as long as the body. It flies, butterfly-like, to search for buds and shoots with juicy plant sap to suck.

STAR FACT

The name "lantern fly" sounds like this insect should give out light – yet these bugs never shine. At first, scientists thought their bright colors meant they could possibly glow in the dark.

Lantern fly

Scientific name: *Fulgora, Pyrops* and others
Type: Insect – hemiptera (true bugs)
Lifespan: Usually 1 year
Size: Up to 3.9 in (10 cm)
Range: Mainly tropical and subtropical forests

HIDDEN...

The bug's bright colors blend in well with tropical flowers for camouflage.

SPECIAL FEATURES

SNOUT: The long rostrum is adapted for extracting highly nutritious juices such as sap and nectar from flowers, buds, stems and fresh leaves.

WINGS: This bug's highly colored wings flash when flying in sunlight, as a way of attracting a mate for courtship.

This bulky, fearsome-looking insect is armed for self-defense. Found only in the wild in New Zealand, the weta is at risk from many kinds of introduced predators, including cats, rats and stoats. During defense it hisses, extends its legs to raise its body, then kicks its rear leg around in an arc with surprising speed and power. Its tough skin covering gives it added protection.

ARMORED KICKER

'STAR FACT

Giant wetas can weigh more than 2.1 ounces (60 g), which makes them one of the heaviest of all insects. These outsized specimens are usually well-fed females ready to lay their developed eggs.

SCRAPE...

The strong mouthparts gnaw and scrape plants and fungi, and they can easily draw blood if they bite a human.

SPECIAL FEATURES

MOVEMENT: Wetas are not great leapers like their grasshopper, katydid and cricket cousins. They tend to crawl and clamber among trees.

DEFENSE: Giant wetas don't have wings and cannot jump well, so they rely on their size and strength during defense against predators.

Giant weta

Scientific name: *Deinacrida*
(several species)
Type: Insect – orthoptera
Lifespan: 5-plus years
Length: Up to 3.9 in (10 cm)
Range: Limited areas of New Zealand

BIGGEST...

The Little Barrier Island weta is the largest of the giant wetas. The name "weta" is derived from a New Zealand Maori phrase meaning "spirit of ugly things."

CLAWS: Each of the six feet end in a set of sharp, powerful claws that grip and dig into bark or wood, making the weta very difficult to dislodge.

SENSES: Big eyes and long antennae enable the weta to move around and feed at night – it is a mainly nocturnal (active at night) insect.

As plant-eating close cousins of crickets and grasshoppers (sometimes called bush-crickets), katydids are best camouflaged among plants by green or brown color schemes. However this bright-pink katydid seems to mimic no plants at all. Its color occurs due to random changes or mutations in the genes, which happen rarely but repeatedly. Peacock katydids are another type, and have folded wings that fan out to show "eye spots" like a peacock's tail.

BRIGHT LEAF

STAR FACT

Rare color variations, or morphs, of leaf katydids are so outlandish in color that they probably survive because predators have never seen anything like them and avoid them.

SLICE...

Katydids have very strong mandibles or "jaws" that work from side to side like shears to snip up plant foods.

SPECIAL FEATURES

ANTENNAE: Katydids are often called long-horned grasshoppers due to their elongated antennae that feel through the undergrowth.

EYES: The large, forward-facing eyes (here reflecting the plants and scene around) provide extremely good depth judgement for leaping.

Leaf katydid

Scientific name: *Orophus* and other species
Type: Insect – orthoptera
Lifespan: 1 year
Size: Up to 3.1 in (8 cm)
Range: Warmer woods and forests

NOW YOU SEE IT...

This leaf-mimic katydid blends superbly into its surroundings – it looks like a faded leaf. The pattern even copies patches of fungus and decay found on real leaves.

WINGS: The front wings have intricate patterns of leaf-like veins providing the insect with extremely realistic camouflage when hiding on leaf litter.

REAR LEGS: Three times longer and 20 times stronger than the front legs, the rear pair can fling the katydid on an impressive leap of more than 9 feet (3 m).

This strange-looking bug has some of the best camouflage in the insect world. Disguised as a leafy twig, the giant prickly stick insect of Australia has an array of large and small spines and spikes over most of its body. Only the female is huge and prickly – the male is hardly half the length, slimmer and less spiky. Yet its camouflage is still top class, and both the female and male will remain hidden if a predator comes near.

SPIKES GALORE

'STAR FACT

If there are no males around for mating, the female stick insect can still lay eggs that hatch into female babies. Female-only reproduction is known as parthenogenesis.

DEFENSE...

The stick insect may arch its tail over its back when disturbed to resemble a venomous scorpion – but it is harmless.

SPECIAL FEATURES

EGGS: The female doesn't take care of her eggs. They are simply flicked from her body and scattered on the forest floor below.

LARVAE: Ants collect the eggs to eat their tasty outer coverings. When the grubs hatch they run from the ants' nests into the trees.

Giant prickly stick insect

Scientific name: *Extatosoma tiaratum*
Type: Insect – phasmid
Lifespan: 2–3 years
Length: Females up to 7.9 in (20 cm)
Range: Forests of Australia and New Guinea

HARD TO SPOT...

Stick insects can range in color from almost black to green, brown, yellow and grayish-white. Each chooses a background, such as a dead leaf to match its own color.

WINGS: The females do have small wings, but they cannot fly as well as the males. The males' wings are longer and stronger, so they fly to search for a mate.

CAMOUFLAGE: Leaf-like body parts help this insect blend in with surrounding twigs and leaves. If a breeze moves the foliage, the insect sways too.

The tail of this bug looks like it could give a nasty sting – but any resemblance to a real scorpion is accidental. The male scorpionfly has a curved rear end with a sharp, fierce-looking "stinger" at the tip. But this is not a weapon and has no venom. Instead, it is used to hold onto the female scorpionfly during mating. Female scorpionflies will attack hopeful males unless they are tempted with an attractive offering of food.

FAKE STINGER

STAR FACT

The male scorpionfly has a risky courtship, as the female may stab him with her long mouthparts. He spits some saliva onto a leaf for her to lap up during mating.

PRESENT TIME...

Some types of male scorpionfly catch a fly, butterfly or similar "gift" to attract and give to the female. This makes it less likely she will attack him.

SPECIAL FEATURES

ANTENNAE: These bugs tap foliage with their antennae to detect traces of possible insect prey in the form of scent trails and droppings.

MOUTHPARTS: The long "beak" has strong mouthparts, called mandibles, which can bite through small insects.

HIDE...

The four long, lacy wings are patterned with spots and blotches to help camouflage the insect as it crawls over plants, and during flight.

Scorpionfly

Scientific name: *Panorpa* and others
Type: Insect – mecoptera
Lifespan: Usually 1 year
Wingspan: 1.1-1.4 in (30-35 mm)
Range: Mainly temperate woods

TAIL: The male's tail is often held arched over the back like a real scorpion's tail, but it is harmless and used for mating, not stinging.

PARASITIC FEEDING: Scorpionflies sometimes sneak near spiders' webs and try to steal the owner's dead, wrapped-up victims.

In the heavy, humid night of the Central American jungle, a long, bendy shape darts across a rock. The tropical giant centipede is out on the prowl. Its feelers dab the ground and sweep the air for faint scents of small creatures, while its legs detect any tiny vibrations through the ground. An unwary mouse emerges from its nest hole and in a split second the centipede's fangs have stabbed in their venom, and the hunter starts its meal.

FATAL FANGS

STAR FACT

The female giant centipede is among the few creepy-crawlies that show parental care. She guards her eggs and rubs them to prevent them going moldy.

SPECIAL FEATURES

BODY: The bug's long body consists of about 22 segments, which are all very similar – apart from the head and the fanged segment at the front.

LEGS: Centipedes have one pair of legs per body segment – millipedes have two. They move in a coordinated, wave-like motion from front to back.

Giant centipede

Scientific name: *Scolopendra, Melopendra* and others
Type: Myriapod – chilopod
Lifespan: 5–10 years
Size: Up to 11.8 in (30 cm) long
Range: Tropical America, Caribbean

ATTACK...

This centipede can attack many kinds of prey, from bugs and worms to frogs, lizards, mice, birds, bats and even tarantulas!

PIERCE...

The giant centipede's sharp fangs are usually held just below the head. They extend forwards and move apart, then come together fast and hard to bite.

FANGS: The front pair of legs, called forcipules, have adapted into fangs, which allow the insect to jab its victims with a potent, paralyzing venom.

VENOM: This centipede's venom is deadly enough to kill its prey. It is hardly ever fatal to humans, but causes great pain, swelling, fever and sickness.

It's spring in the woods and the trees are crawling with cicadas. The males chirp and screech so loudly that other animals hide from the noise. After many years underground as nymphs (grubs), feeding on plant roots and similar matter, these insects all emerge and molt into adults at once. Millions of them flutter, clamber, sing, mate and lay eggs, but the noise doesn't last for long – a week or two later, their short adult lives have ended.

MASS CHOIR

Periodic cicada

Scientific name: Magicicada (several species)
Type: Insect – hemiptera
Lifespan: Up to 17 years
Size: Up to 1.2 in (3 cm)
Range: Eastern North American woods

'STAR FACT

Some types of cicadas live underground as nymphs for just a few years. Periodic cicadas manage 13 years in some areas, and even 17 years in others! All develop into adults over the same few weeks.

MOLT...

The nymphs climb up plant stems and their body casings split. The adults climb out, their wings ready to expand.

SPECIAL FEATURES

EMERGENCE: These bugs all emerge from their tunnels when the soil temperature reaches 60.8-64.4°F (16-18°C). The timing of this varies from place to place.

SINGING: Cicadas make deafening chirps by vibrating flexible patches of skin, called tymbals, on the sides of their abdomens.

By day, the two-spined spider hides from its predators under leaves and on twigs. The extraordinary raised lumps on its abdomen brilliantly disguise its otherwise rounded shape. At night it spins a web, which usually lies horizontally (flat) rather than upright. Crouching nearby, the spider waits for a meal, such as a tasty gnat, to fly into the web.

SPINY HUNTER

STAR FACT

Female two-spined spiders have horns, bright colors and wide bodies. Yet the males are less than half the size, thin and dull in color. They were once thought to be a different species.

Two-spined spider

Scientific name: *Poecilopachys austalasiae*
Type: Arachnid – araneida
Lifespan: 3-4 years
Size: Females 0.3 in (8 mm) long, males 0.1 in (3 mm)
Range: Australian woods

TRAP...

The two-spined spider spins a wheel-shaped orb web and specializes in catching small moths and flies.

SPECIAL FEATURES

SPINES: The spines or horns are sharp-tipped and work as camouflage to break up the spider's shape, making it look like a thorny plant.

COLORS: This is one of the few types of spider that can change its colors to match its surroundings.

Rhinoceros beetles are named after their long nose horns, and the hercules beetle is champion among them for horn length. Only the males have the large horns on the front of the head. They are used in trials of strength at breeding time. The adult beetles live for just a few months, after spending two years as grubs, tunneling through and eating old, rotting wood.

HUGE HORNS

LIFT...

For its size, the hercules beetle is one of the strongest animals. It can lift more than 800 times its own body weight.

STAR FACT

Hercules beetles primarily use their horns to fight rival males and impress females. They interlock horns, push and shove, try to lift and slam down their opponent – and even try to snap off their head!

SPECIAL FEATURES

UPPER HORN: This is an extension of the shield-like covering over the thorax (middle body section), which protects the legs and wings.

LOWER HORN: The shorter, more "toothed" lower horn may help grip a rival when struggling to lift and decapitate him.

Hercules beetle

Scientific name: *Dynastes hercules*
Type: Insect – coleoptera
Lifespan: 2–2.5 years
Size: Males up to 7.9 in (20 cm), including horns
Range: Central and South American rainforests

NOSE-DIVE...

The long horns and weighty head shield make the beetle front-heavy in flight. If threatened it usually prefers to crawl away, or rear up, kick out and jab with its horns.

MOUTHPARTS: The powerful mouthparts can chew through tough plant foods – although the hercules beetle prefers soft, rotting fruits and berries.

HAIRS: The upper horn's fringe of hairs, and hairs on the head and body, may help to detect vibrations and air currents made by approaching predators.

Cunning, surprise and efficient killing equipment are the main needs of a successful predator. The assassin bug is an expert killer and it lurks among undergrowth or between rocks, waiting patiently for its next target to come past. Without warning it dashes from its ambush hideout, sprinting on its long legs. Then it unfolds its long proboscis, which is both a sharp-tipped dagger and a tubelike drinking straw, and plunges it into the victim.

CLEVER KILLER

WEAPON...

The long mouthparts, or proboscis, are usually folded under the head, as shown here, beneath the many-sectioned eye. The pointed proboscis tip is extremely hard.

SPECIAL FEATURES

COLOR: Most assassin bugs are drab in color. This gives them superb camouflage in their habitats, which are mostly woods and forests.

LEGS: The long, strong legs kick at the ground as the bug moves, so it is able to accelerate quickly when necessary.

Assassin bug

Scientific name: *Rhinocornis,*
Reduvius and many others
Type: Insect – hemiptera
Lifespan: 2–3 years
Lenth: Up to 2.4 in (6 cm)
Range: Tropical and subtropical forests

STAR FACT

Some kinds of assassin bugs clamber onto spiders' webs and flick the strands as though trapped. When the spider arrives to investigate, the bug jumps up, bites it to death and starts to eat.

STAB...

An assassin bug often strikes at the thorax of its victim, such as a bee, to immobilize its wings and legs so it cannot escape.

PROBOSCIS: The mouthpart muscles are very powerful and jab the cone-shaped tip easily into most animals – even tough-cased beetles.

FEEDING: The assassin bug dribbles digestive juices through its mouth tube into the meal, usually a small insect, then sucks up its blood and body fluids.

Despite being an inoffensive sap-sucker, the bizarre-looking peanut bug has developed a number of weird ways to put off predators and camouflage itself. One ploy is to bob its nut-shaped snout up and down. The snout is reptile-like, with prominent eyes (giving this insect an alternative name of "alligator-headed bug"). A predator might mistake it for the bobbing head of a lizard or snake. Since the snout is mostly hollow, moving it does not take much muscle power.

NUTTY DISGUISE

WEIRD...

One theory for the peanut bug's strange-shaped snout is that when the insect stands at an angle on a branch, it resembles an old, lichen-covered, broken twig stump.

SPECIAL FEATURES

PATTERNS: The fake eye patterns about one-third from the base of the peanut bug's snout may distract any nearby predators.

EYES: The bug's true eyes are near the base of the snout and have sharp vision to spot airborne hunters, such as birds and bats.

Peanut bug

Scientific name: *Fulgora laternaria* and closely related species
Type: Insect – hemiptera (true bugs)
Lifespan: 1-2 years
Length: 2.8-3.1 in (7-8 cm)
Range: Central and South American forests

'STAR FACT

The peanut bug may suddenly move its two front wings aside to reveal startling "eye spots" on the rear pair. These look like the staring eyes of a cat, owl or similar predator, and frighten away enemies.

BLEND...

When the large, butterfly-like wings are folded, they blend in perfectly with mossy, lichen-covered branches.

SMELL: This bug can give off a strong, horrible smell, similar to a skunk's stink, to put off mammal predators such as tree rats and shrews.

SOUND: The bug may bash its head on its tree perch to make a drumming sound that confuses approaching hunters.

Blue weevils are not just blue – some are pale, some dark, others greeny blue, gray blue, sky blue or midnight blue. This extraordinary range of colors depends on the exact genes inherited by each weevil from its parents. Whatever the exact shade of blue, predators such as birds, lizards and shrews know that this unnatural color, for an animal, signals danger. The weevil tastes horrible, so predators soon learn to leave it alone.

TINY POISONER

UP AND AWAY...

Most weevils can fly well using their larger rear pair of wings (the front pair are specialized as wing covers). This view shows the long rostrum stretched forwards.

SPECIAL FEATURES

ANTENNAE: The feelers have ultra-fine hairs that respond to the slightest air movements, helping the tiny weevil to fly steadily in wind.

SNOUT: Weevils are beetles with an elongated, drawn-out rostrum used to probe into flowers, buds and similar plant foods.

Blue weevil

Scientific name: *Eupholus nickerli*
Type: Insect − coleoptera
Lifespan: 1 year
Size: 0.2 in (5 mm)
Range: Most habitats, especially warm forests

'STAR FACT

There are more species of insect than any other animal group, and there are more types of beetle than any other insect. With more than 50,000 species, weevils are the largest animal family on Earth.

GOBBLE...

All weevils eat plant foods and some kinds are serious crop pests, devastating human plant foods and products.

TOXINS: The weevil's flesh and body parts contain several kinds of toxins (poisons) that make any creature who eats it feel sick and dizzy.

COLOR: The dazzling blue hue acts as a warning. If a predator eats one weevil, it feels so ill it avoids them in the future, helping the whole species.

Along a tropical tree twig, this colorful creature moves more like a slug than an insect. It seems to wiggle along on its belly rather than walk, but this caterpillar is a true insect – it is the young stage, or larva, of the slug moth. Its main task in life is to eat, while protecting itself with an impressive defense display. As a predator nears, the fleshy lumps on the caterpillar unfurl to reveal long, sharp hairs loaded with nasty stinging chemicals.

TOXIC CRAWLER

BASH...

Some very hungry birds may bash, slap and wipe slug caterpillars on a branch to remove as many hairs as possible, before swallowing.

SPECIAL FEATURES

HEAD: The caterpillar usually keeps its head bent low, under a fold of the front body, so it is less noticeable.

COLORS: The dazzling red, yellow and purple warning colors signify to predators that this caterpillar is best avoided.

Red slug caterpillar

Scientific name: *Setora fletcheri*
Type: Insect – lepidoptera
Lifespan: 1 year
Length: Up to 2 in (5 cm)
Range: Tropical, especially Southeast Asia

DISGUISE...

STAR FACT

One of the main chemicals in slug caterpillar hairs is histamine – a substance found naturally in the human body that causes inflammation, redness, swelling and itching.

The adult moths of slug caterpillars are expertly camouflaged. This green-leaf fairy slug moth mimics a fallen leaf with edges turned up and going brown.

HAIRS: The caterpillar's hairs are sharp but weak and brittle. They puncture the skin and snap easily to release their irritant chemicals into flesh.

HAIR BASES: Fleshy mounds called tubercles carry the bunched hairs, and expand to fan them out when the caterpillar senses danger.

GLOSSARY

adaptation a change in a type of animal that makes it better able to live in its surroundings

ambush a surprise attack

antenna a feeler on the head of some animals. The plural of "antenna" is "antennae."

camouflage colors or shapes in animals that allow them to blend with their surroundings

forage to go from place to place looking for food

irritant something that causes discomfort to the body

mandible a mouthpart of insects or arachnids used to bite or hold food

nocturnal active at night

thorax the section of an insect's body that contains the heart and lungs

vibration a rapid movement back and forth

FOR MORE INFORMATION

BOOKS

Bailey, Jill. *Bug Dictionary: An A to Z of Insects and Creepy Crawlies*. New York, NY: Scholastic, 2003.

Murawskia, Darlyne. *Ultimate Bugopedia: The Most Complete Bug Reference Ever*. Washington, DC: National Geographic Children's Books, 2013.

WEBSITES

Bugs
http://animals.nationalgeographic.com/animals/bugs/
Find many facts and photos of interesting insects on this site.

Bug Facts
http://www.bugfacts.net/
Read more about some of the most common North American insects.

INDEX